GERMAN PAINTING

THE OLD MASTERS

GERMAN PAINTING

THE OLD MASTERS

by Alfred Werner

McGRAW-HILL BOOK COMPANY

New York   Toronto   London   Sydney

For a list of other titles in this series, see page 48

GERMAN PAINTING

The visual arts know no national boundaries. Even in the Middle Ages, when traveling was a painfully slow and often hazardous endeavor, artists from the German territories in Central Europe went abroad for apprenticeship to Roger van der Weyden, to the brothers Van Eyck in Flanders and to the masters of the Early Renaissance in Italy. Later, around 1500, hardly any German master of note failed to spend time studying abroad: Dürer twice visited Italy, and his work reveals the invigorating stimuli received from what he saw and experienced in Venice. Holbein's technique as a draftsman derived to a large extent from Jean Clouet. He ultimately settled in England, and as a portraitist he became so much a part of British civilization that he is often included in books on English art.

So it is difficult to write on German art of the past as though it were an entity sharply distinguishable from art produced in neighboring countries. For instance, it seems true that German painters more often than not expressed themselves in a small format, unlike many of their colleagues south of the Alps who preferred monumental dimensions. Yet is not Grünewald's Isenheim Altarpiece overwhelming in its magnitude? Early German art is generally considered expressionistic to the point of being formless and brutal, albeit of great emotional strength. Yet we also have the works of the Cologne School that are reminiscent of French art of the same period in their quiet, lyrical refinement.

It can be said, however, that panel painting—as distinct from mural or miniature painting—developed relatively late in Central Europe. Master Bertram of Minden, who was born around 1340 and cannot be traced after 1415, was a fairly isolated phenomenon (a fascinating narrator, he painted the stories of the Scriptures in large altarpieces in a lively, naive manner). While we know something about this master, who was active in and around Hamburg, most early German painters are identified in histories of art by artificial names, minted by historians who assemble a list of paintings they consider attributable to an individual master whose name has been lost in the course of centuries and may, perhaps, never be traced through documents, for the practice of signing paintings did not become general in the German lands before the age of Dürer and Cranach. Thus we have a "Master of Saint Veronica" (after a picture of this saint in Munich's Alte Pinakothek) and a "Master of the Life of Mary" (derived from a series of pictures depicting episodes from the life of the Virgin). An artist who was both a painter and an engraver is known to scholars by two "names": as the "Master of the House Book" (a manuscript he illustrated with many pen drawings) and as the "Master of the Amsterdam Print Room" (most of his rare prints are there). However, it does not follow that masters whose names we do not know were inferior to those whose names have been uncovered or invented, or that pictures for which there are no clues whatsoever are less important than those for which essential documentation has been found.

Several impediments to the growth of the arts in the German lands might be mentioned here. In the North to a larger extent than in the South or West, the artist, in the eyes of a still late medieval society, was a mere craftsman, an artisan without personal aesthetic preferences who, like a bricklayer or mason, performed a task for which he was paid like any other workman. The idea of the artist as an inspired instrument developed in the North only in the Renaissance days of Dürer, who portrayed himself as a superior being and was an intimate of the writers and scholars of Nuremberg. But even Dürer had to admit that in Italy, artists were treated with greater respect than in his native country. In the last of his letters from Venice, he writes sadly about his imminent departure from Italy: "Oh, how I shall shiver, longing for the sun: here I am a gentleman, at home a parasite."

Germany had fewer art patrons than Italy; men like Cardinal Albrecht von Brandenburg, who used the skills of the best artists of his time (among them Dürer and Cranach) to adorn his art collection, were not a frequent phenomenon north of the Alps, where religion and warfare were the main preoccupations. There was also much destruction of works of art, first through the iconoclastic fury of the Reformation (though Luther himself was not a foe of the arts), and thereafter during the turmoil of the Thirty Years War. So widespread, indeed, was the destruction that it is safe to assume that we know only a fraction of the art produced in Germany prior to the middle of the seventeenth century. Finally, German art, though at times it reached what we now consider remarkable peaks, never received the attention given to the Italian masters. For a long time the only German masters popularly known outside Germany were Dürer and Holbein the Younger. Even in Germany, interest in German art developed only in the early nineteenth century, with the rise of the Romantic Movement. The very study of German art has been much handicapped by the absence of an early historian who could have done for the Germans what Vasari has done for the Italians or Van Mander for the artists of the Low Countries. Joachim von Sandrart's seventeenth century compilation of artists' biographies was no more than a mélange of gossip and anecdote. It was he who referred to the great artist as "Grünewald" although, according to the identity established in 1917, he was actually named

Figure 2. Stephan Lochner: St. Jerome in His Study. North Carolina Museum of Art, Raleigh

5

*Figure 3. Swabian School,
circa 1470: The Two Lovers.
The Cleveland Museum of Art,
Delia E. Holden Fund
and L. E. Holden Fund*

Matthias Gothardt Neithardt. It is, by the way, significant that until the last century the celebrated Isenheim Altarpiece was thought to be the work, not of the half-forgotten "Grünewald," but of Albrecht Dürer.

In this volume we are concerned with what might be called the "Golden Age" of German art, the one hundred-odd years that reach from Stephan Lochner to Hans Holbein the Younger. Split into countless petty feudal states, religious or secular, Germany did not develop what might be called a national style either before, during, or after this period. It is in fact not quite accurate to speak of German art as such before the nineteenth century. Instead, there were various regional schools—Rhenish, Westphalian, Swabian, Lower Saxon, and so forth—that filled the large area between Hamburg in the North and Bozen (Bolzano) in the South, Colmar in the West and Prague in the East. Do the pictures produced there, have a common denominator? They emphasize, by and large, the romantic, mystical, irrational elements in religion and life to such a degree that one is tempted to set them in opposition to the more rational, more formal, more classic concepts developed elsewhere, particularly in Italy. At the same time the Gothic style—which in some places lingered into the sixteenth century—was international in character. In the northwest—the Lower Rhineland— the Franco-Flemish influence prevailed, while the South (Swabia and Bavaria) derived much inspiration from the art that penetrated from Northern Italy. It is an easy game to establish similarities to Giotto and his circle in one picture, and in another to note a German artist's familiarity with the Van Eycks. Rarely, however, are these influences so overwhelming as to snuff out all Germanic characteristics.

While in Italy, history, allegory and ancient mythology quickly gained a place, and portraiture was widely practiced at an early date, in German lands non-religious subject matter appeared very late. Taking Christianity very seriously, German artists painted, sometimes with extraordinary skill and an unquestionable originality, scenes of Christ's Passion, the Life of the Virgin, and the lives of the various saints. A German Madonna, painted by Konrad von Soest, Stephan Lochner, or Martin Schongauer never achieves the idealized beauty of an Italian Madonna; the German model is, almost invariably, a homely, large-boned, plain-featured Hausfrau. Yet she deeply breathes the passion of maternal love, of Christian devotion. If a generalization can be offered as a hint rather than as an all-embracing formula, it might be said that the German artist placed greater trust in the truth of his religious faith as an artistic guide than in the creative instinct that calls for emphasis on "significant form." Looking at the thousands of surviving fragments of Early, High and Late Gothic German altarpieces, one is not surprised to hear a connoisseur of Classic art dismiss all of them as "barbaric," "primitive" or "naive."

But even the classic writer Goethe could exclaim, "Gefuehl ist alles"—feeling is all that counts. He who treasures the render-

Figure 4.
Northwest German Master:
Little Wing Altar.
Wallraf-Richartz Museum, Cologne

7

Figure 5. *Master Francke:*
Birth of Christ,
from the Thomas Altar,
Kunsthalle, Hamburg

ing of intense feelings above all else will be rewarded by the manner in which Germany's early painters managed to express suffering and grief in Crucifixions that in their stark "realism" do not spare the onlooker. Violent action and ugly faces surround Christ in Johann Koerbecke's *The Taking of Christ.* Master Francke's *Christ Bearing the Cross* excels in unpleasant realistic details that anticipate the much later Grünewald. But the same Master Francke was able, in another panel of the St. Thomas Altar, to depict the Adoration of the Child with the utmost tenderness, giving the scene a fairy-tale character. Thus it is inaccurate to equate early German art with "Expressionism." In the Archbishopric of Cologne, that "Rome of the North," one of the best of early fifteenth century artists, Stephan Lochner, was employed. Of what has been called "German harshness," little is left in the lyrically delicate, tender and wistfully gentle Madonnas painted there by men who knew that this world was not always a valley of tears. In the region of the Upper Rhine (probably at Basel) the celebrated *Garden of Eden* was painted. The very young Madonna is seated reading a book; the Holy Child, amused by the sounds of a zither, is attended by a young saint, possibly Cecilia; the other saintly personages are enjoying themselves in a garden filled with flowers, bushes and trees, with a dozen birds resting on twigs, on the crenellated low walls in the background, or flying through the crisp blue air. Nothing more cheerful was painted throughout the century, nothing more colorful.

The long period from around 1330 to 1470—from "primitive" masters who decorated the churches in Cologne to the highly skilled Schongauer, creator of the *Madonna of the Rose Garden,* in Colmar—was one of considerable change. Slowly but inevitably, the Byzantine gold backgrounds in pictures gave way to interiors of rooms and even landscapes. Gradually both artist and society abandoned contempt for this world and craving for the next and became reconciled with reality. Within the course of a few decades, stiff, rigidly linear figures that were little more than generic types began to give way to full-blooded, plausible earthy beings that moved naturally through a three-dimensional space. At a certain point, a chronicler narrates, "The world began to live again and be cheerful and people ordered new clothes for themselves."

Two masters in particular stand at the watershed between medieval idealism and that new realism that allowed Germans to benefit from the achievements of the Renaissance south of the Alps. One was Lukas Moser, a Swabian to whom only one work, dated 1431, the St. Magdalen Altar in the parochial church of Tiefenbrunn (near Pforzheim) can be attributed with any certainty. On the frame, the artist put this tragic exclamation: "Cry, Oh art, and bewail, for no one, alas, will have any more of you now." This statement has been interpreted to mean that Moser deplored the growing unpopularity of the traditional art in which he had grown up. Yet paradoxically, he himself, through his own work, helped introduce the feeling for reality and nature, for plastic synthesis that was to transform German art completely before his century was over. Mary Magdalen washing the feet of Christ; the voyage of the Saint and her companions to Marseille, and all her other adventures, are treated with a realism resembling Flemish painting of the period that so curiously emphasized the patterns made by the ocean's waves and details in distant mountains and valleys.

Figure 6.   Konrad Witz:
The Miraculous Draught of Fishes.
Musée d'Art et d'Histoire, Geneva

An even more daring man was his Swiss contemporary, Konrad Witz whose *Miraculous Draught of Fishes* contained the first real landscape in European panel painting (landscapes had appeared earlier only in illuminated manuscripts). Witz was the first painter to put men into a world where water, trees and rocks were real. Moreover, it is not an invented landscape. Witz had painted the actual port of Geneva, with Mont Blanc in the background (*See Figure 6*); he had conquered distance with a skill unparalleled in early fifteenth century art.

Unfortunately, American public collections today offer the student little opportunity to acquaint himself with the splendor of early German painting. This is largely because in the nineteenth century, when American millionaires bought everything that the market could yield, it was fashionable to concentrate on the great names, especially Dürer, Cranach and Holbein. Thus we have here now a half dozen Dürers, and a great many Cranachs and Holbeins (though Cranach's early, still medieval and romantic work was neglected). But the USA owns no large German altarpieces and no works by Lochner or Witz. This lack is an echo of Anglo-American opinion of pre-1450 German art, dismissed in older handbooks as "stiff, uncouth, devoid of ideal beauty: angular; archaic, ugly."

Yet the German precursors of Dürer were as talented as were the Italian precursors of Titian. Today nobody anywhere considers pre-Dürer art crude or technically inept. If a German "Primitive" were up for auction at New York's Parke-Bernet Galleries, or at Sotheby's in London, American museums would outdo each other in bidding for it. We have new eyes for this old art, and we have learned to appreciate the bright, transparent colors, the unhackneyed forms, whether gross or slender, and above all, the devotional piety that emanates from them. And a singular characteristic of the saintly figure is that he is frequently enveloped in a rich costume, resplendent with velvet, silk, gold and brocade, that contrasts strangely with his unwordly expression, the gentle inward look.

But however remarkable German painting was in the fifteenth century, undoubtedly the climax was reached in the century to follow—more precisely, in the years from around 1500 to 1550. For in this period, or during most of it, four men were active whose names can be mentioned together with those of Raphael, El Greco, Rembrandt or Poussin. They are, in chronological order; Matthias (or Mathis) Grünewald, Albrecht Dürer, Lucas Cranach the Elder and Hans Holbein the Younger. Grünewald, the religious painter, master of the haunting reds and greens, the dark sky and the celestial light, actually never bore this name as mentioned earlier. But this fictitious name apparently cannot be eradicated and will probably continue to be used even in standard works.

Survive, too, will the legends woven around him and incorporated in numerous novels and in Hindemith's opera (Mathis der Maler), all taking for granted that the artist led a lonely life ("ein eingezogenes Leben") and that he was unhappily married ("uebel verheiratet"), as Sandrart reported. All we can be certain about regarding his family life is that he had an adopted son. A courtier like Matthias could not possibly have led a "withdrawn" life, and it is surprising still to read in serious monographs that he was a portraitist and engraver, and the teacher of Dürer, none of which can be proven.

This, then, is in brief, the story of Matthias' life: he was born at Wuerzburg around 1460. As a court painter to the archbishop of Mainz (whose residence was at Aschaffenburg), Matthias had a regular salary, his own coat of arms, costly robes and, undoubtedly, many responsibilities. He accompanied his master on his travels, for instance, to Aachen for the coronation of the new emperor, and it was there that Matthias and Dürer briefly met. Commissions led the painter to a number of places, notably to Isenheim in southern Alsace, where he produced his most famous work, the polyptych originally installed in the church of a religious order caring for the severely ill, but eventually transferred to what became known as the Musée de Unterlinden in the nearby city of Colmar.

Suspected of Lutheran sympathies, Matthias lost his position in 1526. In his two remaining years he proved his versatility by being a soapmaker in Frankfurt, and a hydraulic engineer in charge of the municipal water works of Halle, where he died. An inventory of his estate revealed that, far from having suffered poverty, he had owned valuable clothes and jewelry. That he harbored "subversive" ideas seems to have been established by Lutheran writings found among his possessions.

To see his principal work, one has to take the journey to the remote city of Colmar, far off the trodden routes. Works by Grünewald can also be studied and admired in museums of Munich, Frankfurt, Karlsruhe, and other German cities. But it is not sufficiently known that, apart from a minor chalk drawing kept in this country by a private collector, the United States has a genuine and very valuable Grünewald; the small crucifixion that is part of the Kress Collection in Washington's National Gallery of Art.

Surprisingly, the French have had the highest respect for this so un-French, so utterly Germanic artist. A contemporary of the great Wilhelm von Bode, the French novelist Huysmans engaged in dithyrambic praise of the Isenheim masterpiece. Another great tribute comes from Elie Faure: "He (Grünewald) knows how to give to his color the accent of the drama, how to agitate, harrow, and terrify one. He is as tragic as he is trivial; he is cruel, sinister and drunk with strength and horror." The French peacemakers even wrote the polyptych into the Versailles Treaty to make sure that it would be returned from Munich—where it was except during World War I—to Alsace!

Is it correct to say that Grünewald is typically German? Christian Zervos, the friend and biographer of Picasso, does not think so. He feels that Grünewald's work contains the essence of human suffering without reference to a particular race, nation or creed:

"He is not of any nationality nor of any school. He is neither Greek nor Gothic, Dutch nor Italian. He is all of them at once, for he is Grünewald."

The same idea is expressed by Nicholas Pevsner, who hails Grünewald as "one of the greatest masters of European painting," not of German painting alone.

On the other hand, it is safe to say that Grünewald was a precursor of those German Expressionists who helped to revolutionize art in the beginning of this century. Max Beckmann's love for Grünewald is well known; Heinrich Nauen was clearly influenced by him; and there is an affinity between him and Nolde, Kokoschka and others, whether or not they ever actually saw his work in the original.

Whereas Grünewald was an isolated figure who probably never left German territory, Dürer was a well-traveled European, with friends in the most illustrious circles. Attempts to turn Dürer into a super-German had been made long before the rise of Hitler, but they had been disparaged by conscientious scholars like Heinrich Woelfflin who insisted that Dürer journeyed to Italy because he expected to find there the artistic liberation that he sought, or Valentin Scherer who remarked that, although Dürer's art found a Germanic expression, its appeal was certainly universal.

In this country, paintings by Dürer can be found in the Metropolitan Museum, the National Gallery, and in the Philadelphia Museum of Art, while New York's Morgan Library has a number of his drawings and prints. Yet the "Da Vinci of the North," the "Columbus of German Art" has not yet become so familiar in America as the titans of the Italian Renaissance. The story of this denizen of the free Imperial city of Nuremberg and protégé of Emperor Maximilian I is known to every German school boy. There is much in his personality to endear him to

Figure 7. Albrecht Dürer: Portrait of Hieronymus Holzschuher. Berlin-Dahlem Museum

14

Americans as well. He managed at one and the same time to be a matter-of-fact traveler and businessman as well as a lonely experimenter and thinker. A genuinely modern man, he was the first German conscious of being an artist instead of "an honest craftsman who produces pictures as a tailor makes coats and suits" (Erwin Panofsky). He was the first to draw or paint the countenances of wife, parents and friends. He signed (with his famous monogram) and dated not only his finished works, but a good many sketches, though they were not intended for sale. Held in high esteem by many outstanding and influential men, he accepted all forms of admiration with artistocratic poise. Indeed, he was the first German to elevate himself gradually from the humble status of a more or less anonymous medieval craftsman to that of a patrician, on equal footing with men of great power and wealth.

He dared to talk back to patrons—a thing that even in our own day not every artist feels free and strong enough to do. For instance, when the patrician Jacob Heller, who had commissioned an altarpiece and, in the widely known manner of patrons of the artist, dealt with Dürer rather arbitrarily, the master retorted gently but firmly, refuting the accusation that he had failed to keep his promises:

"From such a slander each and everyone exempts me, for I bear myself, I trust, so as to take my stand amongst other straightforward men . . . I know that when the picture is finished all artists will be pleased with it. It will not be valued at less than 300 florins. I would not paint another like it for three times the price agreed, for I neglect myself for it, suffer loss, and earn anything but thanks from you."

Excepting Michelangelo, Dürer is the only artist of the distant past whose personality we know well, not only from his pictures, but from his writings as well. Even if these writings had been lost—and what a deprivation that would have been—we would still know from his work his affection for his parents. He

was especially devoted to his father, the goldsmith Albrecht Dürer and he twice painted him, an earnest man with strong features and a fine high forehead (pictures in the Uffizi, Florence, and the National Gallery, London). Dürer described his father as a man who "passed his life in great toil and stern, hard labor, having nothing for his support save what he earned with his hand for himself and his wife and his children; so that he had little enough." The famous son added: "But he won just praise from all who knew him, for he lived an honorable, Christian life, was a man patient of spirit, mild and peaceable to all, and very thankful towards God. For himself he had little need of company and worldly pleasures; he was also of few words and was a Godfearing man."

The artist's mother, Barbara Dürer, is known to us from his sketch (in the Berlin Museum's Print Room) made of her when she was sixty-three. Before Dürer, only beautiful young women turn up on the pages of illuminated manuscripts or on panels. It took artists a long time to discover that there is beauty in old age too. Dürer was one of these discoverers who refused to find beauty only in youth, one who, a century before Rembrandt, believed that real beauty was more a matter of character than of appearance. He sketched Frau Dürer—who bore her husband no fewer than eighteen children—when she was emaciated and worn-out, and he paid loving attention to every nuance in her bony peasant face. He also left us a written account of her death, saying that she "bore no malice" even though she had suffered "great poverty, scorn, contempt, mocking words, terrors, and great adversities."

Dürer is often regarded as a serene, well-adjusted intellectual who skillfully adapted to his own needs the achievements of the new area. This is not correct. Dürer appeals to us so strongly because, like us, he was full of unrest, doubt, anxiety. "What beauty is I do not know," he once confessed, as would any sincere artist living today, "but it adheres to many things."

While many people believe they know what beauty is, Dürer, in genuine humility, broke out in a cry of despair: "God only knoweth what is the perfect figure of a man, and He knoweth likewise to whom He revealeth it." Nothing is further from his mind than the arrogant attitude of those in the nineteen thirties who were to establish a canon of form to which all artists had to adhere, and who destroyed as "degenerate" everything that deviated from their own concept of beauty. "A fine work of art

Figure 9. Albrecht Dürer:
Madonna and Child.
National Gallery
of Art, Washington, D.C.
Samuel H. Kress Collection

17

is well-pleasing to God," Dürer maintains, and he adds: "He is angry with such as destroy the works of great mastership, for that is bestowed by God alone."

Dürer believed firmly in God, and he never deserted Catholicism, though he greatly admired Martin Luther. But his faith was not the simple one of, say, his mother, for he was the true son of a revolutionary age that, dissatisfied with the existing church, re-examined its tenets. With his monumental paintings that show the four apostles (*Slide 12*), Dürer demonstrated that piety can express itself in different ways. The four figures symbolize the four temperaments—sanguine, choleric, melancholic and phlegmatic—into which contemporary theory divided mankind. But Panofsky correctly defends him against the charge of using the four holy men as an excuse for painting nothing more lofty than the four temperaments:

"What Dürer did was just the opposite: he used the theory of the four temperaments, whose fundamental importance for him and his age need no longer be stressed, for the characterization of four holy men and, by implication, of four basic forms of religious experience."

In his prints Dürer's dividedness can be clearly felt. In the engraving *St. Jerome in His Cell*—we see one facet of Dürer: the Christian scholar who secludes himself for contemplation, the hermit who loves the quiet of his own study into which warm, soft light pours through the windows. But Dürer is also the Knight, in the even more celebrated engraving, who, encountering Death and the Devil, must make his own decisions in a period of great uncertainty. Dürer is also identified with *Melancolia*, the winged figure who supports her head on her hand in a brooding fashion, and Dürer is one of the frightened burghers over whom—in the famous wood-cut—the Four Horsemen of the Apocalypse are riding roughshod.

Again and again Dürer occupied himself with one theme, the Passion of Christ, and he was working on a Passion cycle

Figure 10. Albrecht Dürer: Four Horsemen of the Apocalypse (woodcut from Apocalypse Series)

18

when he died. It is an exclusively Christian theme, yet the way Dürer treated it, it must profoundly stir even the non-Christian or the atheist. This stupendous craftsmanship made his friend, the wise Erasmus of Rotterdam, write:

"What does he (Dürer) not express in monochrome, that is in lines of black? Light, dark, splendor, eminence, depressions: and, although they derive from one single printing, several aspects are presented to the eye of the spectator. These he arranges in the most significant lines, yet if you should add color you would injure the work. And is it not more wonderful to accomplish without the blandishment of color?"

Dürer gave his best in his prints, and of all his works these have had the strongest impact upon the development of modern art, especially in Germany. Ernst Ludwig Kirchner relates that as a young student he made a pilgrimage to Nuremberg, saw the woodcuts of Dürer as well as those of other masters, and then knew what path he had to take. Another member of the artists' association, *Die Bruecke*, the still-living Ernst Heckel, also admired Dürer enthusiastically for his work in black and white. (In his own time, Dürer was, of course, a major influence, numbering among his followers such distinguished names as Grünewald and Baldung Grien.)

This many-sided man also was the author of three books of theoretical essays which he himself illustrated, one a treatise on descriptive geometry, one on fortifications of cities, and one on human proportions. No architect, military engineer or town planner could operate today on the principles of Dürer's treatises, but there is still some stimulus to be obtained from this work. The textbook on measuring with compass and ruler, and the work on the proportions of the human body are of interest to diligent students of mathematics and anthropometry as well as to artists, provided these findings are considered in their historical context.

Dürer sacrificed many years to these scientific and tech-

Figure 11. Hans Baldung Grien: Conversion of St. Paul (woodcut)

nical studies: preoccupied with them, he was unable to carry
out several works of art he had planned. Though he wrote down
his ideas essentially for himself, he also labored for the benefit
of young fellow-artists and for those who would come after him.
He was convinced they would go even further in their race
toward perfection. He begged his readers to bear in mind that
he would never have undertaken the task had any textbooks
been available:

"I myself had rather hear and read a learned man and one
famous in his art than write of it myself, being unlearned."

This is not the voice of false modesty. This was written in genuine humility:

"If we want to sharpen our reason by learning and to practice ourselves therein, having once found the right path we may, step by step, seek, learn, comprehend, and finally teach and attain unto something true. Wherefore, he that understandeth how to learn somewhat in his leisure time, whereby he may most certainly be enabled to honor God, and to do what is useful both for himself and others, that man does well: and we know that in this wise he will gain much experience in art and will be able to make known its truth for our good. He that joyfully doeth so, upon him shall much be bestowed by God, from which we receive all things. He hath the highest praise."

Lucas Cranach the Elder is an equally important master. But he lacks the mystical expression of the color-intoxicated Grünewald, the Renaissance sophistication of Dürer, and Holbein's uncannily shrewd insight into human nature. Cranach's color is sometimes shrill and his composition awkward. Besides, his output was so fantastically large that quality had to suffer, and quite a few of the oils attributed to him are probably inferior products of his workshop.

We know that he was born in 1472 in the town of Kronach in Upper Franconia—a region that also produced Grünewald and Dürer—as the son of an obscure painter from whom he received his first training. His mother was the daughter of a shoemaker, but we are not certain of the family's name. After 1500 he traveled a great deal through the Danubian lands, and he may have derived from this journey, which terminated in Vienna, his romantic feeling for landscape. He was known as "Lucas Cranach" when, in 1504, Frederick the Wise, Elector of Saxony, appointed him painter to the court (*pictor ducalis*) at Wittenberg. Unlike so many artists, who prefer constant change and drift from place to place, Cranach was a stable and unadventurous man: he retained his position at Wittenberg and at Weimar until death removed him nearly fifty years later.

Cranach, whom we know from portraits and self-portraits as a stout man with a powerful square head, a fleshy nose, proud eyes, and a majestic, well-groomed beard, managed to combine the life and attitude of a big businessman with the unceasing pursuit of art. Even before his appointment as court painter he acquired respectability by marrying the daughter of the mayor of Gotha, and he himself subsequently served several terms as

Figure 13.
Lucas Cranach the Elder:
A Prince of Saxony.
National Gallery of Art,
Washington, D.C.
Ralph and Mary Booth Collection

city councilor and burgomaster of Wittenberg. His versatility allowed him to produce hundreds and perhaps thousands of panel paintings (portraits, hunting scenes, religious and allegorical compositions, and the paintings of the female nude) as well as countless woodcuts and engravings. He designed coins and medals for the electoral mint, and with the help of ten assistants, furnished all the décor (including the ornaments of the bridal bed) for the marriage at Torgau of the Elector John the Constant, successor to Frederick the Wise. Nor did he hesitate to emblazon escutcheons and shields.

But he also made money by running a tavern, and then a chemist's shop, having the monopoly of the sale of medicines conferred upon him by the duke (the shop, incidentally, continued to function until 1871, when it was destroyed by fire). He also sold Luther's translation of the Bible, and had a printing press which published the Reformer's writings. At the age of fifty-six he was regarded the wealthiest man in Wittenberg, and he had another twenty-five years to acquire further wealth in addition to his salary as a high-ranking employee of the court.

Cranach had three sons, all of whom became artists, and three daughters, all of whom married men of high social standing. He found time to travel to the Netherlands where Emperor Maximilian, the boy who later becames Charles V, sat for him. He was a friend of Martin Luther whom he drew and painted repeatedly, and whose writings he illustrated with caricatures of the popes. As an impartial businessman, he did not discriminate against Catholics, especially such notables as the Duke of Alva and Archbishop Albrecht of Mayence, who commissioned portraits.

Up to the time he was seventy-five Cranach had been spared most of the vicissitudes which plague man; he was still healthy, rich, and the favorite of a benign ruler, nicknamed "The Magnanimous." But in 1547, this prince, having participated in the war of the Protestant League, was defeated and captured by Emperor Charles V and forced to sign the capitulation of Wittenberg. (At Torgau Castle, many works by Cranach were destroyed by Spanish soldiers). The painter, summoned by the Emperor to the encampment at Piesteritz, begged on his knees for kind treatment of the Elector, reminding the Hapsburg ruler of his early sittings as a boy. John Frederick remained in captivity for several years, and during that period Cranach did not, of course, receive his salary as a court painter.

But there was no need for despair, for Cranach had long been a very rich and famous man. Four years later, John Frederick was released from captivity, and was accompanied home by his loyal painter. Weimar became the new residence, and Cranach settled there in a stately house on the market place. Age apparently had little effect on his powers, for the octogenarian started work on a triptych: the center piece represents the Crucifixion, with Luther, open Bible in hand, standing beside the Cross. But Cranach died on October 16, 1553, before he could finish this large work, and it was brought to completion by his son Lucas.

Dürer complained that his colleague, Cranach, could depict the features but not the soul. But if in his later work there is much that appears monotonous and hackneyed, some of his early lyrical and romantic paintings are among the greatest masterpieces of all times. One notes, in particular, the *Rest During the Flight to Egypt*, his earliest picture authenticated by a signature (here by initials; years later his paintings were signed also with a winged serpent, an emblem awarded him by Elector Frederick). Richard Muther calls the painting, which is now in the Berlin Museum, "ein deutsches Waldmaerchen" (i.e. a German fairy-tale). At the edge of a fresh green Germanic forest are seated the Holy Family, with tiny angel musicians (who look like chubby peasant children) ministering to them. In Vienna's Museum there is another famous nature-imbued work, the *Stag Hunt*, which is like a Gothic tapestry, with scores of running animals, hunters, trees, an aristocratic group in a boat on the river, and dreamy medieval buildings on the horizon. (His stags, one of his friends noted admiringly, were "so natural that hounds barked when they saw them.")

If Cranach did not penetrate the human soul as deeply as the introspective Dürer, he had, on the other hand, a highly developed feeling for the sensuous qualities of trees, animals and young women. Even as a religious painter he was not without merit. There is a great power in his early Crucifixion scenes (like the one in Vienna's Schottenstift) with their Gothic distortions and "ugly" features of gnarled figures, but it must be conceded that, in the course of decades, Cranach's religious work grew less and less emotional.

Figure 14.
Lucas Cranach the Elder:
The Stag Hunt. Courtesy,
The Cleveland Museum of Art.

Figure 15.
Lucas Cranach the Elder:
The Stag Hunt (detail).

He was rightly celebrated for his firmly drawn realistic portraits, which have the solidity of sculpture and rival those of Holbein. Thanks to Cranach, we feel we know scores of sixteenth century patricians, scholars and statesmen and their wives, but, above all, the major figures of the German Reformation. These portraits are perhaps more faithful, more photographic renderings of the sitters than those by Dürer who, one surmises, often gave to the men and women who sat for him much of the gentleness and nobility of his own soul. Cranach, however, saw his people exactly as they were: where a man was fat, smug, and self-indulgent, the painter did not bother to discover tender sentiments hidden in some far recess of his soul. He carefully painted the men's expensive fur collars, the ladies' dazzling jewelry. His oils are of so much documentary value that, when, some years ago, a movie on the life of Luther was produced, the painting, *Martin Luther and His Friends,* at the museum in Toledo (Ohio) was consulted to provide authenticity. In this panel, Luther is at the left; the imposing figure in the center foreground is Elector John Frederick: next to him is Zwingli, while at the extreme right is Melanchton.

Oddly, these great figures in the Protestant movement were anything but admirers of the fine arts. Luther, who fondly referred to Cranach as "our dear cousin," could not discover anything at all praiseworthy in the fine arts, we are told by one historian, and Zwingli even persuaded a congress of Protestant churchmen at Zurich to have works of art removed from churches and destroyed. It is perhaps even more strange that a fervent Lutheran like Cranach should have produced so many frankly erotic nudes. But the Electors and their friends, devout Protestants though they were, were also lusty Renaissance men. For them Lucas painted innumerable Eves and Venuses, and especially Lucretias. Dealing with the latter theme, Rembrandt painted a fully clothed young matron with agonized face, stabbing herself after her virtue had been violated. The Dutch painter's Lucretia is a virtuous unhappy woman, whereas for Cranach the theme is only an "excuse" for showing us a sinuous nude or semi-nude figure pointing a precious dagger to her exposed bosom. The artificial pose, and the bland expression on the face make it clear to the beholder that the threat to life is not very serious. New York's Metropolitan Museum has a *Judgment of Paris* (*Slide 15*) in which Paris, awakened by Mercury meets three highly flirtatious nudes.

Yet these pictures never sank to the level of pin-up girls. They were redeemed by a faint addition of humor, and above all by truly aesthetic elements: enamel-like perfection of color and finesse of line. In this country there are quite a few of these little pictures, some not much larger than a small book, and none of them really vulgar or gross. But while the bulk of the Cranachs in this country are in the collections of the very large museums in the East and Middle West (such as New York, Boston, Philadelphia, Washington, Cleveland, Detroit and Chicago), one of the finest paintings Cranach ever produced can be found in a collection that is off the art lover's familiar itinerary. This is the *Cardinal Albrecht as Saint Jerome* (*Slide 14*), a fine picture in the Ringling Museum of Art at Sarasota.

Perhaps Will Durant was right when he lamented: "Cranach might have been greater had he not succeeded so soon and well." But if Cranach was what his tombstone stated as a compliment, *celerrimus pictor*—the fastest painter—fairness concedes that his fast brush and graver managed to produce much that will survive another four hundred years through its inherent charm. More important, however, the romantic and picturesque elements of Cranach's creativity, in the manner of the "Danube School," may be linked to the work of Albrecht Altdorfer and to some extent also to that of Hans Burgkmair.

To a generation nourished on the imaginative fare of the Expressionists, a painter like Hans Holbein the Younger appears less attractive than the three other painters discussed here. A man who could design anything from initial letters to altar-pieces, he was as versatile as any of the three, and he surpassed Dürer in the quantity, if not quality, of the portraits he produced. But he used his enormous gifts in a cooly commercial manner that was rather alien to such inward directed men as Grünewald and Dürer. Although Cranach also became a calculating businessman, he was a civic-minded individual with social responsibilities.

We must acknowledge and even admire the classical balance, the grandeur of conception in Holbein's painting, incomparable in crystalline clarity. At the same time, we sense a deliberate suppression of imagination: he drew and painted, with cool detachment, what was before him, and nothing else. It is quite possible that Holbein wound up as a shrewd portrait manufacturer because he had seen his own father—a late Gothic painter of great merit—reduced to misery. Shocked by his father's lack of success, he was still in his teens when he left his native Augsburg, accompanied by his brother Ambrosius, for Basel where he hoped to get work from the city's numerous printers of illustrated books.

In Basel, he did obtain the desired commissions (among other things, he illustrated an edition of Erasmus' *Praise of Folly*). He also undertook important mural work. Whether he married Elsbeth Schmidt, the widow of a tanner, mainly for her fortune we do not know. But we do know that he left her and the two children she had borne him, to spend two years in England. He returned to Basel, fathered two more children, and again left his family to go to England, this time for good, except for one brief visit. It is said that in Basel he had a far from platonic relationship with Magdalena Offenburg, who posed for him repeatedly, and whom Rudolf and Margot Wittkower have described as "a beautiful woman of noble family but easy virtue, which brought her into conflict with the law."

We do not know exactly what the chronicler, Joachim von Sandrart meant when he remarked that in England the favor of King Henry VIII was "steadily on the increase, since he (Holbein) amused him in all ways," but it can be assumed that the court painter, who fathered two illegitimate children in London, did not live a monastic life in Tudor England. From another source we learn that Holbein was given to ostentation: "When he visited Basel from England for a short time (a reference to his last stay in Basel) he was clothed in satin and silks—he who formerly had to buy his wine at the tap." Yet though he must have learned a great deal during his second, eleven year-long sojourn in England—during which he painted a large variety of articles of every day use—he must have lived very imprudently to die as poor as he actually did. As we know from his last will, "John Holbeine, servaunte to the Kynges Magesty" left only a horse, plus certain articles from the sale of which some small debts were to be paid: only seven shillings and sixpence per month were left for the support of his two illegitimate children. The wife and four children in Basel are passed over in silence.

But far more bewildering than Holbein's private life is his cynical and opportunistic attitude towards his magnanimous protector, Sir Thomas More. When Holbein first came to England, introduced to Sir Thomas by a letter of recommendation from the scholar Erasmus, it was the then Lord Chancellor of Henry VIII who gave shelter and employment to the German artist, and it was More who introduced Holbein to the king. Yet when Henry VIII invited Holbein to become his court painter, the artist was eager to serve the man who, on a trumped-up charge of treason, had had Sir Thomas thrown into the Tower and finally executed. Holbein managed to the very end to remain in the good graces of the fickle and capricious monarch.

It is true that few remember the biographies of artists while walking from picture to picture in the world's celebrated galleries. Yet in the case of the younger Holbein one wonders whether this unbelievably gifted artist who towered very high above the colleagues of his own generation—he was born in 1497 or 1498 and died suddenly of the plague in 1543—could not have made wiser use of what Fortune had showered upon him. For what survives of his early work—religious paintings, portraits and prints—reveals him as a man capable of work not opposed to what Grünewald, Dürer and Cranach had endeavored to achieve. While there is much of the Italian Renaissance in the altarpieces surviving from the years 1515 to 1526, the Germanic note, that is to say, the romantic, mystical approach of late Gothic art is not altogether missing. For the English Holbein, landscapes do not exist, not even as backgrounds. If there is a background, the figure is placed in a luxuriously decorated Tudor room. Yet the young Holbein was capable of depicting, in his religious paintings, Alpine scenes with high mountains, meadows, rivers and quaint villages.

If one were asked to name *the* picture in which Holbein's genius found its purest expression, one would readily choose *Christ in the Tomb* (Basel) signed and dated MDXXI. H.H., though it is very different from his more celebrated works such as the portraits of Henry VIII and his wives. This long, narrow panel must have been the predella for one of the several altarpieces Holbein produced in Switzerland, none of which have been preserved completely. On the predella of the Isenheim Altarpiece, Grünewald shows us the dead Christ beside the sarcophagus, mourned by the Virgin, Saint John, and Mary Magdelen. Holbein portrays death too, but nothing else; stretched out on a stone slab is a lank body with a ghastly face, glazed eyes and an open mouth. One cannot agree with Paul Ganz who claims that this picture is "lacking all spiritual values." Dostoievsky, seeing this *Christ* in the Basel Museum, exclaimed: "This picture could rob many a man of his faith." A picture without spiritual values would not have moved the Russian novelist so profoundly: *Vanitas vanitatum* seems to be written all over this unforgettable picture with which Holbein for the first and only time ventured into the regions of a much older and more introspective master, Grünewald.

This is not the British Holbein who in each portrait seems to proclaim: "Whatever you wanted me to do—to leave out shadows, to emphasize every detail in your costume, to pay special attention to your jewelry—I have done well, for you paid me handsomely." This Holbein was still a man rather than a perfect painting machine. He was still able to look reverently at individuals who caused his deep respect. Witness his portraits of the wise Erasmus, the "doctor universalis," whom he liked to paint in the solitude of his study, writing, or holding a book. Here is nothing of the tightness and decorativeness of his later work. Here, in a casual composition of warm blended colors, the intellectual authority of sixteenth century Europe is at ease in a quiet atmosphere, gently surrendering to the loving eye of a

Figure 18.
Hans Holbein the Younger:
Sir Thomas More.
The Frick Collection, New York

Figure 19.
Hans Holbein the Younger:
Sir Thomas Cromwell.
The Frick Collection, New York

clever young man. One is reminded of Dr. Johnson's dictum: "Portrait painting is a reasonable and natural consequence of affection." In other words, the best portrait is done whenever there exists an intimacy between the artist and the sitter, a kind of collaboration between the two, a strong personal bond uniting the two characters.

The height of personal statement is reached in the Basel picture *The Artist's Family* which Holbein painted after returning from his first, rather lengthy stay in England.

One writer calls this picture a "masterly self-indictment." Possibly Holbein, at that instance, felt guilty about having spent two years away from his family to "pick up a few shillings" (the phrase occurs in Erasmus' letter of recommendation to Sir Thomas More). There is nothing shocking about Holbein's return to England in 1532; after all, there had been iconoclastic riots in Basel, and Protestant opposition to art made it difficult to prosper there as a painter. But could not Holbein have sent for his family of five as soon as he knew that once more success was knocking at his gates? And this he knew quite soon, for it quickly became the proper thing for the rich German merchants in London to have their likenesses painted by their renowned compatriot. Georg Gisze from Danzig was among these sitters. He appears as a handsome young man with vivid eyes, but Holbein tells us more about his desk and his office than about the man's soul. In the portrait of Hermann Wedish, a Cologne merchant who moved to England, the elegant cloak is painted with virtuosity (the picture is now in New York's Metropolitan Museum), but the facial expression is reduced to arrogant self-confidence. Dürer would have discovered other traits as well, and Rembrandt (or, in our day, Kokoschka) would have revealed emotions concealed by an overly proud front.

Soon high-ranking Englishmen wanted to be painted by this "Apelles of the North." Among the more interesting of the early sitters was Thomas Cromwell, Master of the Jewel house. In quick succession Cromwell became secretary to Henry VIII, Lord Chancellor and Earl of Essex, yet he too, was beheaded in the Tower after the king needed him no longer. Holbein, appointed official court painter in 1536, repeatedly painted the crafty, overbearing monarch in all his barbaric splendor: he painted Henry's third, fourth, and fifth wife, the Prince of Wales, the king's falconer, the master of the horse, and the court physician.

Without Holbein, we would know much less about English high society in the early sixteenth century. But do his portraits belong in a history of art? Are they not to a greater degree part of a history of culture? For the differences in facial expression of both men and women in these pictures are as small as the variety in fascinating appurtenances and other details is large. Perhaps Holbein was not permitted to deviate in the slightest manner from the approved standards of beauty and decorum.

Perhaps he, who gave us little beyond the outward aspect of his sitters, came to feel the way his great successor, Gainsborough was to feel at the height of his career. "I'm sick of portraits," the eighteenth century master wrote to a friend, "and wish very much to take my viol-da-gamba and walk off to some sweet village, where I can paint landskips and enjoy the fag-end of life in quietness and ease."

It is not known whether the practical-minded Holbein—who it seems always needed cash very badly—ever wasted time on "landskips." But it is likely that, tired of painting faces, he had a bit of fun doing the accessories—a magnificent carpet, musical instruments, a jeweled crucifix or mitre, a precious dagger, a falcon, a squirrel, or pink carnations in a vase.

After Holbein, no major personality was to turn up in sixteenth century German painting. The Swabian Christoph Amberger (ca. 1500-1561) might be compared to Holbein insofar as he, too, devoted himself almost exclusively to the art of portraiture; Amberger knew and emulated the Venetian masters whose rich color he used to paint Emperor Charles V, as well as the great bankers of Augsburg. Johann Rottenhammer (1564-1623) also admired Tintoretto and Veronese, and painted his small mythological studies in the Italianate manner. Adam Elsheimer (1559-1610) was another minor master; in Venice, he fell under the spell of Tintoretto, while in Rome Caravaggio was his model. He became famous for his landscapes in which biblical or mythological figures appear amidst dramatic contrasts of light and shade. But none of these three can be said to have been an innovator of any sort, and those who followed them chronologically were even of lesser importance. German art was not to produce any significant painters until the final decades of the nineteenth century in which were born the men who banded together under the name of *Die Bruecke* (The Bridge) and who were to revitalize German painting after a decline of more than three hundred years.

· 1 ·

STEPHAN LOCHNER

(ca. 1400–1451)
Madonna in a Rose Bower
Panel, 19¾″ x 15¾″
Wallraf-Richartz Museum,
Cologne

Against a still medieval gold background, the Virgin Mary is shown in a bower of climbing vines and roses and lilies in full bloom. She is a demure, young person, with a dreamy and remote expression, and holds the Babe on her knee. Around the holy pair crowd tiny angels with out-spread wings. They are bringing gifts or making music on a variety of instruments. High above, in the upper corners, two angels are holding open a gold-brocaded curtain to reveal God the Father and the Dove; the Virgin is robed entirely in dark, luminous blue, and the adoring angels wear red, pink, blue and yellow garments. The grass in the fore-ground is starred with tiny flowers. Note the meticulously painted minia-ture framed in pearls adorning the Madonna's bosom.

While the picture is basically Gothic—the idealized posture of the Virgin, the stylization of flowers, leaves and grass, the traditional gold background—the draping of the blue mantle suggests substance and depth and forecasts future developments in German painting. It is one of the finest pictures done in the Rhineland in the early fifteenth century and is characteristic of a manner of painting which stressed sweetness, balance, and order in a fervently religion-oriented world of hope and happiness. Among the painters of this Rhenish school, Stephen Lochner was foremost in the handling of volumes, the modeling of gracefully rounded faces, and the rendering of details with delicate precision.

· 2 ·

KONRAD WITZ

(1400/1410–ca. 1466)
Annunciation
(ca. 1400–1445)
Panel, 62⅜″ x 48″
Germanisches Nationalmuseum,
Nuremberg

Like all pictures titled "Annunciation" this one shows the archangel Gabriel telling the Virgin Mary that she will give birth to the son of God. Here the angel appears, not in the usual marble-columned hall or cathe-dral apse, but in the kind of simple, middle-class room with timbered ceil-ing familiar to the painter. The Virgin, clad in very full, glowingly greenish-blue robes, is reading a book. The solemn angel sinks upon one knee as he enters. Holding a scroll in his left hand, he points upward with his right. The Virgin has turned toward him without, however, actually looking at him.

Konrad Witz in this picture—one of the few of his authenticated works—superbly renders the importance of the situation by the intensity of expression in the somewhat mask-like faces of his *dramatis personae* and in the quiet solemnity of their attitudes and gestures (the significant language of the eyes, the telling pose of the angel, the magnificent folds of the garments). No words are exchanged, the lips are closed, yet the world-shaking message can be heard.

Considering the early date of the picture, it is remarkable with what skill the artist was able to render the surface appearance of inanimate objects, the atmosphere around the figures, the shadows playing on walls and flagstones and, through excellent perspective, the feeling for space.

· 3 ·

MARTIN SCHONGAUER
(ca. 1445–1491)
Nativity
Panel, 10¼″ x 6¾″
Alte Pinakothek, Munich

The Virgin, in a bright red gown and mantle, sits with the Holy Child on her lap, holding a flower which she may have plucked from the many flowers that adorn the knoll upon which she rests. Youthful and charming, she wears her voluminous robes with grace. In the stable where Christ was born, Joseph stands beside a donkey and an ox. The background is filled with a high Alpine landscape.

While Martin Schongauer is noted particularly for his powerful engravings with their tight linear quality, the few paintings that can be attributed to him are admirable for a combination of delicacy and richness that related him to the more sculpturesque Flemish paintings of his time which he is known to have studied.

· 4 ·

MICHAEL PACHER
(died in 1498)
*Saint Augustine and
Saint Gregory*
(1483)
Each Panel: 81⅛″ x 35⅝″
Alte Pinakothek, Munich

These are the two central panels of an altarpiece painted for a convent church near Brixen (now Bressanone) in Southern Tyrol. This "Altarpiece of the Church Fathers" is Michael Pacher's masterpiece; Saint Jerome, Saint Augustine, Saint Gregory and Saint Ambrose are presented in heroic size, each with his own symbol. The two central panels show Saint Augustine with a child trying to scoop up the ocean with a spoon, and Saint Gregory with the Roman emperor Trajan, redeemed from the fires of Hell through his intercession. They are seated in Gothic niches adorned with elaborate carvings and small statuettes of the apostles, each of whom bears the instrument of his martyrdom. Faces and hands are painted with exquisite care, and the Fathers are highly individualized. Seated under canopies, on episcopal thrones, with the Dove of the Holy Ghost hovering over them, they are noble men, full of serene wisdom, the artist having achieved this grandeur despite a certain stiffness and angularity of forms.

· 5 ·

MATTHIAS
GRÜNEWALD
(ca. 1460–1528)
The Mocking of Christ
(1503)
Panel, 42⅞″ x 28⅞″
Alte Pinakothek, Munich

One of Master Matthias' earlier works, this painting heralds the flowingly dramatic color and emotional intensity of the Isenheim Altarpiece. Howling soldiers surround the blindfolded Son of God, whose hands are tied, while blood is dripping from his face. The two torturers are bursting with fury. An odd figure is the piper in the background whose right hand is beating a drum. Among those sadistic men, however, there is one filled with pity: the bearded man in a turban who, hand on the shoulder of the fat ruffian, seems to be interceding on behalf of the seated figure of the suffering Christ. This pleader has been interpreted as the Scriptures' Joseph of Arimathea. Note the two crossing diagonals that hold the composition together, one of them ending in the tragic figure of the mocked Christ.

· 6 ·

MATTHIAS
GRÜNEWALD
(ca. 1460–1528)
Crucifixion
Detail from the
Isenheim Altarpiece
(1510–1515)
Panel, 106″ x 121″
Museum Unterlinden, Colmar

This altarpiece, composed of a shrine, two fixed and four moveable wings and a predella (a long narrow panel which forms the base), offered different views on the high holidays, Sundays, or weekdays. On weekdays, the Crucifixion looked out from the closed shrine on to the worshippers. The altarpiece was commissioned by the Antonite order for the hospital they maintained at Isenheim, near Colmar, in Alsace. The patients were afflicted with a skin disease called St. Anthony's Fire, and were considered incurable. On admission, every patient was brought to the altar in the hope of a miracle.

Standing out against the mysterious black background, the oversized body of Christ, drained of all blood, seems already decomposing. To the right is the robust figure of Saint John the Baptist who points to the Savior. Below is the white-fleeced, symbolical Easter Lamb, whose blood runs into a golden goblet. To the left Mary Magdalene is seen kneeling on the ground and wringing her hands in distress. On the salve box by her side is inscribed the date, 1515. Saint John the Evangelist is supporting the swooning Mother.

Never before has the tragedy of the Crucifixion been portrayed in the anguished spasmodic manner of this work with its dramatically dark background. The clapsed hands of the Virgin at the left and the Magdalene at the foot of the cross, betray a twitching nervousness that is aptly reflected in the agonized fingers of the Lord. To the extent that Christ is shown covered with the sores of St. Anthony's Fire, it would almost appear that this painting symbolizes the agony of mankind itself.

This profoundly moving picture has been commented upon by many writers. Noting that this polyptych, housed in a Colmar museum since the French Revolution (when it barely escaped destruction), has become "the mecca of an uninterrupted stream of pilgrims," Pierre Schmitt adds: "May these pilgrims never forget that this work transcends all frontiers and racial divisions, and is a part of the artistic patrimony of the whole world."

· 7 ·

MATTHIAS
GRÜNEWALD
(ca. 1460–1528)
Angel Concert and Nativity
Detail from the
Isenheim Altarpiece
(1510–1515)
Panel, 104⅛″ x 119⅝″
Museum Unterlinden, Colmar

This picture, on the inner pair of movable wings and revealed when these are closed, contains two scenes. To the right, seated in a garden, the Virgin, draped in a scarlet robe, and a dark blue cloak clapsed by a precious brooch, looks happily at the Babe she is holding in her arms. In the foreground are a cradle, a small bowl and a small wash tub. Red roses emerge beside the Virgin. In the background one notes a lake with deep blue water, a monastery and, behind it, a wood and mountains. High in the sky, God the Father, surrounded by numerous angels, reveals himself in a stream of light.

The left part of the picture is occupied by a glittering Gothic room in which a group of angels are singing. In the foreground, three angels are playing instruments; the first, red-robed, plays the viola; the second, in a robe made of green feathers, the bass-viol; the third, whose garments are white, the viola di gamba. The colors and objects, as is usual in Northern European painting, generally have meanings far beyond their everyday relationship to the story itself. Thus, red in the case of the Virgin's robe, symbolizes her suffering; while the presence of such commonplace objects as the wash tub refers to her purity.

· 8 ·

MATTHIAS
GRÜNEWALD
(ca. 1460–1528)
St. Erasmus and St. Maurice
(1520–1525)
Panel, 89″ x 69¼″
Alte Pinakothek, Munich

This panel is part of an altarpiece that was commissioned by Cardinal Albrecht von Brandenburg for the Collegiate Church of Saint Maurice and Saint Mary Magadelen in Halle. To the left stands the earnest and dignified Bishop Erasmus, in his episcopal vestments, accompanied by a bareheaded, tired-looking canon. (Erasmus is given the features of the donor, Cardinal Albrecht.)

To the right is the Negro Saint Maurice, the lively and gesticulating leader of the Theban Legion, who wears shining armor. He is followed by a retinue of archers and lancers. The two major figures are invested with halos as insignia of their sainthood. At Erasmus' feet are the heraldic devices of the religious foundations of Mayence, Magdeburg and Halberstadt.

· 9 ·

ALBRECHT DÜRER

(1471–1528)
Portrait of Oswolt Krel
(1499)
Panel, 59½″ x 47⅜″
Alte Pinakothek, Munich

The handsome young sitter, a native of Lindau, was the Nuremberg representative of a Regensburg firm of merchants. Three years after the picture was painted, he returned to his native city which he served eight times as burgomaster. Albrecht Dürer, who painted this portrait at the age of twenty-eight, skillfully concentrated on rendering the man's powerful character by emphasizing the ardent gaze of his fiery eyes, a feature of many of Dürer's subjects as witness the famous portraits of Jerome Holzschuher, the fiery glance of the Saint on the right in Dürer's *The Four Apostles* (*Slide 12*), and the intense stare in the drawn portrait of Dürer's mother (*Figure 8*). This device of the intent look or fiery glance of the sitter, in principle, distinguishes the portraits of Dürer from those of most of his contemporaries.

Expressively painted, too, are the long curly hair and the texture of the fur. The more decorative elements are the background of glowing red and, in a narrow strip at the left, a bit of imaginery landscape.

· 10 ·

ALBRECHT DÜRER

(1471–1528)
Adoration of the Magi
(1504)
Panel, 37⅞″ x 44⅞″
Uffizi Gallery, Florence

This picture is believed to be the central portion of an altarpiece, the wings of which are in the museums of Frankfort, Cologne, and Munich. It was commissioned by Dürer's faithful patron, the Elector Frederick the Wise, and originally placed in the court chapel at Wittenberg. For many years the picture belonged to the Hapsburg's gallery in Vienna, but in the eighteenth century it came to the Uffizi, in exchange for a picture by an Italian master.

The title refers to the three Oriental wise men (or kings) who visited the Christ Child and presented Him with gifts. To the left is Mary, a fair-haired German Hausfrau robed in blue; she presents her child to the kiss of the eldest of the three. Right of center is the Moorish magus or king, between two arches; behind him is a strongly illuminated hill. Every detail in this picture is drawn with great strength and precision as befits one of the great engravers of all time. But this highly detailed treatment, typical of this age in Northern Europe is balanced by Dürer's conscious attempt to achieve large-scale geometrical arrangements in his composition suggesting the art of the contemporary High Renaissance in Italy. Thus, a painting of this type exemplifies the combination of Germanic detail and emotional intensity on the one hand, and Italian monumentality on the other. It is not for nothing that Dürer was known as the "ambassador of the Italian Renaissance to Northern Europe."

· 11 ·

ALBRECHT DÜRER
(1471–1528)
Portrait of Michael Wolgemut
(1516)
Panel, 11½″ x 10½″
Germanisches Nationalmuseum,
Nuremberg

Michael Wolgemut (1434-1519) was well-known in Nuremberg for his paintings and woodcuts, and altogether an important figure in German fifteenth-century art. After having learned the craft of the goldsmith, young Albrecht Dürer was apprenticed to Wolgemut and stayed with him for more than three years. Though he was to develop a style totally different from that of his master, Dürer throughout his life continued to hold his teacher in high regard. Here Wolgemut is shown at the age of eighty-two; his features are sharp and bony, his nose is aquiline, his skin shriveled. Despite his old age, Wolgemut looks into the world with energetic, clear eyes. As in the portrait of Oswolt Krel, the fur is painted with superb realism. The inscription, by Dürer, was made in two stages: the first refers to the act of painting in 1516; the second was added after the old man's death: ". . . when he passed away on St. Andrew's Day, early, before the sun rose." Dürer survived his master by nine years only.

· 12 ·

ALBRECHT DÜRER
(1471–1528)
The Four Apostles
Left Panel: St. John and
St. Peter, 85″ x 30″
Right Panel: St. Mark and
St. Paul, 85″ x 30″
(1526)
Alte Pinakothek, Munich

This picture, which was to be his last major work, was donated by Dürer to the Nuremberg Senate in the same year in which it was painted, and was placed in the voting chamber of the City Hall. In 1627 it was presented by the Senate to the Elector Maximilian as a "token of esteem." Although the title, *The Four Apostles*, has come to be generally accepted, it is not accurate, for Saint Mark, the Evangelist, was not an apostle. Dürer is known to have painted this picture as an expression of faith in the old-time religion, as opposed to tenets held by the growing numbers of sectarians and doubters. This becomes clear from reading the texts, suggested by Dürer, and set down at the bottom by a calligrapher named Neudoerffer (using extracts from the Holy Writ, these lines are meant to combat those who were threatening the established faith and order).

These monumental, statuesque figures also, according to tradition, represent the four temperaments: John, who is absorbed in contemplation, is melancholy; Peter, phlegmatic; Mark, sanguine; and Saint Paul, choleric. Apart from their meaning, these panels have always been admired for their powerful colors and for the master's inimitable grasp of form.

Coming after his final visit to Italy, and indeed painted within two years of the artist's death, *The Four Apostles*, like the much earlier *Adoration of the Magi* (Slide 10), brings together the emotional tensions of Germanic painting with the breadth of High Renaissance art: in this case, the nobly expressed drapery folds of the great Giovanni Bellini who had befriended Dürer during the famous Venetian visit.

41

· 13 ·

LUCAS CRANACH
(1472–1553)
Portrait of Johann Stephan Reuss
(1503)
Panel 21½″ x 15″
Germanisches Nationalmuseum,
Nuremberg

This is one of Cranach's earlier works. The sitter was an eminent jurist who became rector of the University of Vienna a year after this portrait was painted (Reuss died in 1514). A portrait of Reuss' wife, also done by Lukas Cranach the Elder, is preserved in the museum at Berlin-Dahlem. The inscription at the top indicates that Reuss was forty-one when he sat for his portrait. Reuss wears a red cap and a fur-lined red garment. His hands, adorned with rings, are on the pages of an open book. In the background is a typical Cranach landscape with interesting trees, a castle, and jagged mountains, all in a tranquil light. This kind of reserved portraiture is related to that of the young Holbein; far from being spontaneous, it outlines the grave, self-aware features of the scholar with sober objectivity and sound naturalism.

· 14 ·

LUCAS CRANACH
(1472–1553)
*Cardinal Albrecht von
Brandenburg as St. Jerome
in His Studio*
(1526)
Panel, 49″ x 32″
John and Mable Ringling
Museum of Art,
Sarasota, Florida

The pomp-loving prince, who was a great supporter of the arts, employed Cranach between 1520 and 1526. Cranach often painted his patron, twice as Saint Jerome against an open landscape, and twice in his study. Here, the Cardinal appears in the guise of the animal-loving Saint, who is translating the Bible into Latin—the version called the Vulgate—in the presence of a menagerie that includes, of course, his faithful lion. It was not far-fetched to present this particular Cardinal as Jerome, since Albrecht von Brandenburg was, indeed, a humanist who encouraged the writer Ulrich von Hutten and corresponded with the Erasmus of Rotterdam. When he retired from his favorite residence, Halle, to Aschaffenburg, to escape from the Reformation and from his creditors, he took along his various art treasures.

Note how Cranach was able to suggest space. On the wall with a window hangs one of his characteristic Madonnas. On the table is a cardinal's hat. In its arrangement, the picture is, undoubtedly, indebted to Albrecht Dürer's engraving of 1515, *St. Jerome in His Study*.

· 15 ·

LUCAS CRANACH
(1472–1553)
The Judgment of Paris
Panel, 40⅛" x 28"
The Metropolitan Museum
of Art, New York
Rogers Fund, 1928

This particular theme goes back, not to Homer's epic, but to a medieval novel derived from it. According to this story, Paris the Trojan prince, went hunting and was lost in a deep wood. He bound his horse to a tree, then fell asleep. To the sleeping man appeared Mercury who brought with him three Goddesses—Athena, Minerva and Venus—and asked Paris to decide which of them was the fairest.

Cranach and his numerous assistants produced for the court of Wittenberg, and other aristocratic customers, many "Scenes from Antiquity" like this in which the somewhat mannered male figures wore sixteenth century garments and armor, while the females were, for the most part, in the nude. Here, the three young women are long-limbed, slender and graceful figures; all wear heavy necklaces, the one in the center also wears a large hat and a narrow diaphanous veil. Note the Cupid, with bow and arrow in the upper left and the castle on the strangely shaped rock in the upper right.

· 16 ·

LUCAS CRANACH
(1472–1553)
*Venus with Cupid as a
Honey Thief*
Painted after 1537
Panel, 69" x 26"
Germanisches Nationalmuseum,
Nuremberg

The subject is based on an idyll by the ancient Greek poet, Theocritus, which tells how Cupid complained to his mother Venus of being stung by bees after he had stolen their honey. The Latin quatrain in the upper right corner refers to this incident and ends with a moral: "Like this boy Cupid, we, too, often search for fleeting pleasures which are mixed with pain and cause us only damage."

The courtly—even gallant—picture itself is in sharp contrast to this moralizing lesson, for it is clear that the theme was nothing but a pretext to show an elegant nude Venus wearing nothing but some jewelry and "covered" with an absolutely transparent bit of gauze. She pays little attention to Cupid who is holding up the honeycomb which started the trouble. The scene is set in the kind of dark Northern forest which often appears as background in Cranach's pictures.

43

· 17 ·

HANS BURGKMAIR
(1473–1531)
Saint John in Patmos
(1518)
Panel, 60¼″ x 49⅛″
Alte Pinakothek, Munich

This is the central panel of what was a polyptych or altarpiece composed of many parts. Here Saint John the Apostle, is seen sitting under a palm tree on the Greek island of Patmos, writing. Around him are luxuriant tropical flora and fauna, while in the background is the sea, with tall mountain peaks on its shores. Twisting his neck, the Saint, who had been cast on this strange island, suddenly looks up completely spellbound—a brilliant, many-colored light has burst through the clouds and in the heart of the light appears the Virgin, the Queen of Heaven. Note the rich folds in the Saint's mantle, and the care with which each leaf and each animal has been drawn.

· 18 ·

ALBRECHT ALTDORFER
(ca. 1480–1538)
Landscape of the Danube Valley
(ca. 1520–1525)
Parchment mounted on wood,
11⅞″ x 8⅝″
Alte Pinakothek, Munich

While Dürer had already made quick watercolor studies of landscape after nature, Albrecht Altdorfer is usually credited with being the first painter of pure landscape, from which the human element is omitted. (Earlier, landscape existed only as a backdrop for religious, historical or allegorical action.) Here, a bit of the Upper Danube near Regensburg (Ratisbon) is seen with a castle in the middle background. Altdorfer himself was a native of Regensburg. Anticipating modern landscape painting, Altdorfer managed to treat the landscape atmospherically rather than topographically or geologically. The forest and the sky are painted with a freshness and naturalness never before experienced. The mood of a forest is rendered with astonishing warmth and spontaneity. With Altdorfer, the Germans gained such reputation as landscapists that, as the Italian chronicler, Giorgio Vasari, was to put it, in his time—the middle of the sixteenth century—in Italy there was not a cobbler's booth but was decorated with a German landscape.

The illusion of spatial depth is created through the strong contrast between the tallness of the trees framing the scene at left and right, and the smallness of the castle in the background.

· 19 ·

ALBRECHT ALTDORFER
(ca. 1480–1538)
The Battle of Alexander
(1529)
Panel, 62¼″ x 47¼″
Alte Pinakothek, Munich

The picture's full title runs: "The Battle of Alexander the Great against the Persian King Darius at Issus" (see the inscription, in Latin and German, at the top). This was one of a series of historical scenes commissioned by Duke William IV for his palace in Munich from several artists, including Burgkmair. Napoleon is said to have remarked that this was the best battle picture in existence. He liked it so much that he appropriated it and had it hung in his bathroom at Saint Cloud. After Napoleon's fall the picture was returned to Munich in 1815.

Altdorfer approached his task as if he were a miniaturist. A good magnifying glass will reveal that the thousands of participants in this gigantic battle, Persians and Greeks, are carefully painted. The spectator looks down at the scene. In the center one can observe the personal conflict between the two rulers, both in golden armor. Alexander, on his horse Bucephalus, with his visor up, is pursuing the fleeing Persian king on whose chariot is written: "Darius". The victorious Greeks wear the equipment of German knights, while the fleeing Persians wear Oriental turbans.

While the enemies are locked in deadly combat, sun, winds and clouds seem engaged in a vast cosmic struggle, carried out over the vast plain, the mountains, lakes and archipelagos. The drama of the human forces below is thus echoed by the macrocosmic conflicts in the realm of nature. Although both Greeks and Persians were heathens, to Altdorfer and his patron, this battle at Issus, fought three hundred and thirty-three years before the birth of Christ, as the inscription indicates, appears as a symbol of the victory of Christ.

· 20 ·

HANS BALDUNG GRIEN
(ca. 1480–1545)
Nativity
(1520)
Panel, 41″ x 28″
Alte Pinakothek, Munich

Hans Baldung Grien, who came from Dürer's studio, is known for his delight in painting Holy Family pictures as night scenes, the participants being lighted with an eerie, almost supernatural glow. Here the miracle takes place within the steeply rising walls of castle ruins, with full moonlight coming in through the apertures. A heavy projecting pier divides the picture into two portions. On the left, the disproportionally large ox and ass—the symbolic representatives of the Old and New Testaments—look with earnest eyes upon the touching scene to the right. There, Joseph and Mary are looking down on the tiny Child on the white sheet held by two angels. On the stone steps, three more angels are singing the praise of the Child (from whom the light emanates). In the open door above Mary, the Dove is seen descending in a halo of light, and below a shepherd with a flock of sheep can be seen.

Here the principle of chiaroscuro—the juxtaposition of light and dark—is well applied, as the light dramatically moves from area to area. The picture has the charm of a fairly-tale, enhanced by the creation of a nearly surrealist atmosphere.

45

· 21 ·

HANS BALDUNG GRIEN
(ca. 1480–1545)
Rest on the Flight into Egypt
Panel, 19⅞″ x 15⅜″
Germanisches Nationalmuseum,
Nuremberg

Although this small panel is signed with the monogram of the German artist Schaeuffelin, it is undoubtedly a work of Hans Baldung Grien. Here, the carpenter Joseph, a heavy-set strong peasant type, is bending over a well; next to him is Mary with her Child. They are resting beneath a fir tree, having escaped from Herod's persecutions in Palestine. This is a charming, poetic idyll, seen against the freshness of nature, with a castle on a hill, and high blue mountains in the background. Baldung seems to have loved nature; he received his surname "Grien" from his fondness of the color green. Paintings of this kind illustrate the mixed ancestry of German painting at this time—the pyramidal shape of the Virgin and the face of St. Joseph suggesting contemporary Italian Renaissance painting as does the extended aerial perspective of the landscape. The intensive attention to detail and the romantic character of the tree sheltering the Holy Family suggests, on the other hand, native Germanic tradition.

· 22 ·

HANS HOLBEIN
THE YOUNGER
(1497?–1543)
Portrait of Nikolas Kratzer
(1528)
Panel, 32⅞″ x 26⅜″
Louvre, Paris

This is one of the few portraits that have survived from Hans Holbein's first stay in England (1526-1528). Nicolas Kratzer (1487-1550), native of Munich, entered the service of Henry VIII after having studied at Corpus Christi College in Oxford. He was the "deviser of the King's horologes" and his court astronomer. He also instructed one of the daughters of the king's chancellor, Sir Thomas More, in astronomy.

The artist, a homely man with a large nose and small, yet bright eyes, is seen intently at work. The Latin inscription on the sheet of paper on the table refers to "Nicolai Kratzer monacensis" (i.e., from Munich) and gives his age and the date. In his left hand, Kratzer holds a pair of dividers, and in his right hand a polyhedron of boxwood, with graduated circles engraved on its faces. On the table, on the wall and in a niche are various instruments the scientist would use in pursuit of his work.

Like many of the portraits of this type, the figure is seen sharply silhouetted against a contrasting background which throws the form into impressive relief and gives it its monumental quality.

· 23 ·

HANS HOLBEIN
THE YOUNGER

(1497?–1543)
Madonna with the
Meyer Family
(ca. 1526–1530)
Panel, 56¾″ x 39¾″
Grandducal Castle, Darmstadt

This so-called "Meyer Madonna" is often referred to as "Germany's Sistine Madonna," as it approaches Raphael's celebrated work in dignity and charm. The large picture was commissioned by Jacob Meyer, who served as burgomaster of Basel until his Catholic sympathies led to his party's losing control of the City Council. The picture, for the chapel of Meyer's castle near Basel, was meant as a public profession of the Catholic faith amidst the upsurge of a rising Protestant wave.

The fair-haired and rosy-cheeked Virgin stands in a niche, under a shell-shaped classical canopy. She wears a dark-greenish dress, with golden-hued sleeves. To the left is the kneeling donor, with his two sons (the small one, in his nudity, appears like a little Cupid—or a little John the Baptist). To the right are images of Meyer's first wife (who had been dead when the picture was painted), of his second wife and of the daughter of Meyer's second marriage. The Virgin has the ennobled features of Magdalena Offenburg, a Basel beauty, who posed for several of Holbein's paintings.

It may be of interest to learn that this picture and an almost identical one in the Dresden Gallery were the cause for the so-called Holbein war. For in the second part of the last century, scholars claimed that the "Meyer Madonna" in Dresden was not, as had been believed, by Holbein, but a mere copy. The picture in Dresden is now considered the work of Bartholomaeus Sarburgh, an early seventeenth century artist.

Of all the works of Holbein, this is perhaps the most Italianate as witness the face of the Virgin and the little blond child at the left of the conch-shaped niche in the background.

· 24 ·

HANS HOLBEIN
THE YOUNGER

(1497?–1543)
Edward VI as a Child
Painted before 1540
Panel, 22⅛″ x 17⅞″
National Gallery of Art,
Washington, D. C.
Mellon Collection

Henry VIII often used to step to the window after the end of the day and show his little son, Edward, to the people. Here the two-year-old seems to be waving with his right hand to the acclaiming people. The little boy wears a rose colored doublet and a rich red garment with gold-embroidered sleeves; in his left hand he holds a golden rattle. The picture, presented to the King on January 1, 1540, is listed as a New Year's present in the royal records as "By Hanse Holbeyne a table of the pictour of the P'nce (Prince's) grace."

Although the child was still small, Holbein managed to give him rank and majesty. From his father, Edward inherited his full face and small mouth. The Latin poem was subsequently added on the bottom of the picture; composed by the court poet, Richard Morsin, it admonishes the prince to equal his father in wisdom and virtue and to become the greatest ruler of his age. Unfortunately, Edward had little chance to show what kind of ruler he would make, since as Edward VI he died at sixteen.

For the English speaking world, this painting is of particular interest since it portrays the little prince who is one of the chief characters in Mark Twain's famous novel, "The Prince and the Pauper."